ob 1517

Published by Creative Education
123 South Broad Street, Mankato, Minnesota 56001
Creative Education is an imprint of The Creative Company

Design and production by Stephanie Blumenthal
Printed in the United States of America

Photographs by JLM Visuals (Charlie Crangle, Anthony J. Irving, Joan M. Jacobs, Richard P. Jacobs, Breck P. Kent,
Richard P. Kent, Keith Nicol, Mike Reblin, Doug Reid, Simon R. Young), Eugene G. Schulz, Tom Stack &
Associates (Erwin & Peggy Bauer, Bill Everett, Dave B. Fleetham, J. Lotter, Keith H. Murakami, Mark Newman,
Milton Rand, Greg Vaughn), Unicorn (Jeff Greenberg, Frank Pennington,
Alice M. Prescott, Marshall Prescott, Charles E. Schmidt)

Library of Congress Cataloging-in-Publication Data

Bodden, Valerie.
Volcanoes / by Valerie Bodden.
p. cm. — (Our world)
Includes bibliographical references and index.
ISBN-13 : 978-1-58341-466-8
1. Volcanoes—Juvenile literature. I. Title. II. Series.
QE521.3.B63 2006   551.21—dc22   2005053716

First Edition
2 4 6 8 9 7 5 3 1

OUR WORLD

VOLCANOES

Valerie Bodden

A volcano is a kind of **mountain**. It is a mountain with a big hole in the top! Volcanoes are found all over the world. They are hot inside. Sometimes smoke comes out of the hole in the top. Some people used to think that gods lived inside volcanoes!

Some volcanoes are very big. Others are small. The biggest volcano in the world is called Mauna Loa (MOW-nuh LO-uh). It is in Hawaii.

The holes in the top of volcanoes can be huge

Some volcanoes are covered with rocks. Some of the rocks are small. Others are huge! Lots of volcanoes are covered with snow. It can snow a lot on a volcano!

Deep snow covers the sides of some volcanoes

Trees grow on the sides of some volcanoes. Flowers grow on some volcanoes, too. The dirt on volcanoes is good for trees and flowers. It helps them  grow strong! Flowers can make volcanoes colorful.

Some volcanoes are covered with plants

Sometimes volcanoes erupt. When a volcano erupts, **ash** comes out of the top of the volcano. Some ash is white. Other ash is black. Some ash is gray or brown. The ash rises high into the air.

Volcano ash can be thick

Lava comes out of a volcano when it erupts, too. Lava is orange or red. It is very hot! It looks like fire. Lava shoots up out of some volcanoes. It can shoot high into the sky! Lava flows down the sides of other volcanoes.

Some lava flows slowly over rocks

After lava comes out of a volcano, it cools down. The lava moves slower. Then it gets hard. It turns into rocks. Some of the rocks are black. Other rocks are brown.

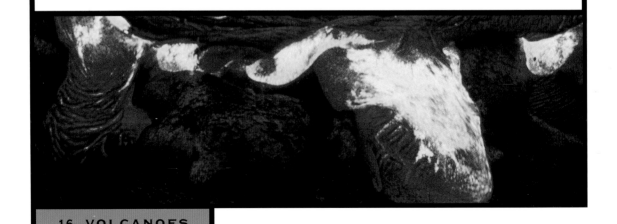

Rocks made from cooled lava are often smooth

*Lava is very hot
and can
burn people*

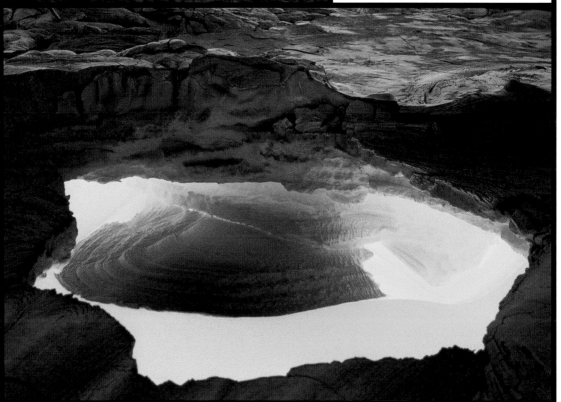

Some volcanoes have not erupted in a long time. Other volcanoes erupt all the time. Some volcanoes are **dangerous** when they erupt. People have to stay away! If they get too close, they could get hurt.

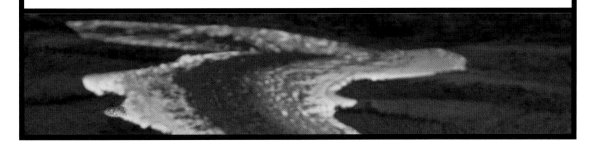

Other volcanoes are safe. Some people stand near the top of these volcanoes. They ride over the volcanoes in helicopters. They even watch lava shoot out of the volcanoes!

Volcanoes can be exciting to watch

Lava flows slower as it cools down. Make your own lava. Have a grown-up help you warm up some syrup. Pour the syrup on waxed paper. Tip the paper. Watch the "lava" move. Let it sit for two hours. Then tip the paper again. Does the cooled lava move faster or slower?

GLOSSARY

ash—very small pieces of rock that come out of volcanoes and float in the air

dangerous—not safe

lava—very hot, melted rock

mountain—a very big hill

LEARN MORE ABOUT VOLCANOES

Hawaii Volcano Photos
http://www.decadevolcano.net/
photos/hawaii_photos.htm

Lava Pictures
http://www.volcanoupdate.com
/LavaPics.htm

VolcanoWorld Kids' Door
http://volcano.und.nodak.edu/
vwdocs/kids/kids.html

INDEX

ash 12
dirt 10
erupt 12, 15, 19
flowers 10
lava 15, 16, 20, 22
Mauna Loa 6
people 5, 19, 20
rocks 8, 16
snow 8
trees 10